G000092779

STORMS OF LIGHT:

A COSMIC AWAKENING.

STEPFANIE GREENER

DISCLAIMER:

The information in this book is not to be used as professional medical advice and is not meant to treat or diagnose medical problems.

Copyright © 2022 by Stepfanie Greener

ISBN13: 9798374190816

All rights reserved.

Copyright: No part of this publication may be reproduced without written permission from the author, except by a reviewer who may quote brief passages or reproduce illustrations in a review with appropriate credits; nor may any part of this book be reproduced, stored in a retrieval system, or transmitted in any form or by any means – electronic, mechanical, photocopying, recording, or other - without prior written permission of the copyright holder. The trademarks are used without any consent, and the publication of the trademark is without permission or backing by the trademark owner. All trademarks and brands within this book are for clarifying purposes only and are owned by the owners themselves. For permission to publish, distribute or otherwise reproduce this work, please contact the author at stepfaniegreener@icloud.com.

CONTENTS

INTRODUCTION

This book uses creative writing and poetry written over the last 17 years during my spiritual awakening to tell my story of remembrance. You will be taken on an adventure into the dark night of the soul, through healing and into a higher state of consciousness, connecting with the cosmos and 'home' beyond Earth.

I hope those who read it find themselves within the poetry and feel a connected, shared human experience. I also wish to offer hope, even in the darkest of places, to show that no matter how hopeless things may seem, a new reality is always just a moment away.

DEDICATION

To all the truthers, freedom fighters, starseeds and lightworkers that have courageously awakened and stood in your power as the sovereign beings we are meant to be. It hasn't been easy and many have lost everything, all apart from what is most important; LOVE, UNITY and FREEDOM.

I am proud to be a part of the revolution and creation of the new Earth alongside you all. It's been a long hard battle, and on the surface still appears to continue but do not be mistaken, the light has already won.

Keep fighting the good fight with the most powerful weapons of all; LOVE, PEACE and HIGH VIBRATIONS.

We are one.

FIRST COMES DARKNESS

This journey begins with the dark night of soul. This is a time when our soul becomes truly conscious of its suffering and finally makes a stand to say NO MORE.

This is usually the beginning of a spiritual awakening.

To overcome the dark night, we must acknowledge our pain, be open to feel it fully and make the courageous decision and commitment to heal and transmute it once and for all.

Life is a beautiful dance of duality, within every inner battle we fight, there's a turning point, an opportunity is given for us to acknowledge and accept this ever-present duality. This enables us to learn the lessons being offered, helping us to evolve into a higher state of consciousness.

Nothing is inherently good or bad, everything just is. Even the most negative circumstances are usually fertile grounds for personal and collective growth and ascension leading us to our highest potential.

Always remember that no matter how deep your suffering, there is always hope.

ALWAYS.

Even after death.

You'll see.

DUALITY

At war with myself,
On a merry go round,
Thoughts like knives,
Making so much sound,
I fight against,
I battle real hard,
This weary mind is ever so scarred.

I feel the pain,
It churns all day,
Tensing with angst,
Keeping peace away,
I search for calm,
I'm on the defensive,
This weary stomach is ever so tense.

What can I learn,
I ask inside,
My heart feels heavy,
Much wisdom to provide,
I lean in close,
I open to more,
This weary heart is ever so sore.

What can I do,
To stop despair,
It deepens within,
The more that I care,
I wait for the turn,
I hope for peace,
This weary soul is waiting for release.

It takes a lot,
But redirection comes,
Stamping through leaves,
And dancing to drums,
I see the bright lights,
I feel the love enter,
This spirit is shining, rediscovered its centre.

A new leaf overturned,
After long in the pain,

Inspiration came through,
"What did you gain?"
I found that the presence,
Of darkness and light,
Is what makes a soul so loving and bright.

ROAD TO RUIN (2006)

I'm on the road to ruin,
They're talking again,
Maybe this time, they'll see the pain,

The pain inside,
That cuts me,

Cuts me like a knife,
Only the scars aren't there,
They go so deep,
Who is it that cares?

No one does, as no one can see,
Unless you take a look,
Deep inside of me.

Thoughts,
Like a painful scratching,
Inside my head,

The blood,
Washing away,
What they said,

This cloud,
On my mind,
It's almost like going blind,

I can't see,
The world,
Reality,
Or life, for what it is,

Because, I'm on the road to ruin.

You wouldn't want to know,
It's hell in here,
If you felt only half,
You'd not see clear,

Seeping poison,
Through my veins,

The storm inside,
It rains and rains.

Begging for,
just one short break,
But soon you lay down,
And the pain you take,

At times the pain, becomes too much,
You get lost,
Your spirit is crushed,

Because, you're on the road to ruin.

Trapped in life,
You continue alone,
It's hard to accept,
That this,
Really is your home.

There then comes a point,
A choice you must make,
A chance is given,
For you to take,

You must choose love,

And drop the pain,
To stop insanity,
And become sane,

It's not easy,
But try you must,
This is the journey,
That you should trust.

THE BULLET INSIDE (EGO)

The bullet hits, it's time to frown,
That's when your whole world, comes
  crashing down,
Once it's there, there's no way out,
No matter how much, you scream and shout,

Inside.

Even though, there's love to create,
It doesn't mind, it loves to hate,
It brings you down with force and fear,
No one can care, as no one can hear,

Inside.

After the crash, the strength ignites,
But the bullet then takes you, to the highest
*   heights,*
Yes, it's great, feeling the ecstasy,
But the bullet explodes, so you can't see,

Inside.

After the high, then comes the low,
There really is no place to go,
Wandering around, in despair,
No one understands, so you don't share,

Inside.

So alone you remain, hiding your pain,
Until the bullet subsides, and lets you enjoy
*   the rain,*
You finally jump, off the wheel,
You get some peace, balanced you feel,

Inside.

So yes, the bullets still there, but so it the rain,
You learn to live, and become sane,
Life is balanced, light has returned,
You can live with both, this you've learned.

W hen a soul chooses very painful and traumatic circumstances for its life on Earth it is usually to prepare for a higher calling. It is within the process of experiencing so much darkness and overcoming such painful circumstances that we learn how to hold both extremes of duality within our being. The result of this process allows us to have the natural ability to transmute the darkness in others and the Earth itself, without the use of anything other than our very essence and presence here.

Many starseeds and lightworkers choose to experience deep pain and trauma as it is the most fertile ground to learn and evolve as a human and awaken the light within. This helps us to remember our mission and be the light we came here to be.

Many of us have an uncomfortable urge inside, feeling like we should be doing something profound in life to carry out our mission, or that we need to be helping and reaching as many people as possible, in order to positively impact the world. However, what some don't realise is that they are already making a difference in the world and helping humanity rise just by simply refusing to accept anything that insults their soul, healing themselves, being authentic and living with pure intentions.

It took me a long time to realise this, and finally let go of the feelings of urgency that I'd felt my whole life. I always felt I needed to be doing more to help or that I was 'failing my mission' by not appearing like I was helping people on a large scale. We can forget the level of interconnectedness within humanity and the fact that every time we stand up for what is right, heal something within ourselves or help someone without the motive of personal gain, it is recorded within the collective energy, consequently affecting the world as a whole.

That's how powerful you are.

After a traumatic childhood, I went on to battle with what appeared to be severe mental illness which came in the form of intermittent, life shattering 'psychotic episodes', resulting in terrifying and torturous otherworldly experiences, sometimes lasting up to 9 months at a time trapping me in an eternal hell. These 'episodes' destroyed my life every time in the most catastrophic ways imaginable. On multiple occasions, I was hospitalised, restrained and medicated against my will, losing all my rights and freedoms which turned a divine initiation into an experience of hell. I came to realise that these episodes were part of my soul's remembrance and awakening, and my initiation to become the powerful healer I am today.

The episodes started in 2006 with what would be classed as severe depression but I see it purely as 'emotional agony' as a result of how painful my life felt. These episodes got progressively worse and continued up until 2017 which brought the last and worst of them all. Following this, I stepped away from all of my relationships and finally started to heal myself from the deep trauma that I held inside, which was obviously from personal experiences but also the collective trauma that we all hold, as these cannot be separated.

To the dismay of the doctors, against the odds I always came back stronger than ever after each 'episode'. I refused to accept the 'life long, debilitating and incurable' labels and prognoses I was given, and set out to fulfil my mission and make sure my suffering would not be in vain.

How did I keep coming back from such devastating and hopeless circumstances?

What gave me strength?

What gave me hope?

What kept me on this Earth?

FOR YOU

Before you,
The world was pain,
The scars ran deep,
Everything seemed, in vain,

I was lost from myself,
Didn't know where to start,
To search for what was missing,
From my broken heart,

Then to Earth you came,
To save my soul,
You must have saw,
This world, taking its toll,

I now have a reason,
To stay here and heal,
The pain runs so deep,
Many layers, to peel,

For you, I will do this,
To save you from the pain,
The cycle must stop,
So you won't suffer in vain,

You saved my life,
Just being mine,
Forever I'll be grateful,
Time to heal the ancestral line.

I was sent 2 beautiful children. That's what brought me back every time stronger than ever.

It is important to find our anchor on Earth so we can always find our way back to where we need to be. However, it's just as important to truly *want* to heal and live for OURSELVES and not just for others.

Our children are our greatest teachers. They can give us so much purpose and determination, helping us prioritise our healing.

It is, after all, in the act of healing ourselves that we heal our children and all future generations.

That's how we change the world!

One of the most common triggers that causes us great suffering in life is usually around our relationships with others. Particularly when we have experienced childhood trauma as we will usually find ourselves in unhealthy and abusive relationships as an adult and can get stuck in these cycles for a long time without being able to escape.

Many unfortunately find themselves in situations like this........................

HIM

The highest heaven, to the deepest hell,
From vibrant light, to a crumbling shell,
It starts out wrong, but feels so right,
You had no idea, he would cost you your
      light,

Even when, you see the bad,
No good saying, you'll be made out mad,
He moulds and bends and twists the truth,
But soon you dig, and become a sleuth,

You understand, but aren't understood,
You give it all, but run you should,
Doesn't take long, until all is gone,
It did feel right, now it feels wrong,

Once you know, you plan your escape,
But illusion returns, "maybe it's a mistake?"
You start from scratch, back to heaven
      you go,
You crave this moment, no matter how low,

It's perfection, drenched in blood,
You want to be free, from the sinking mud,
But denial takes over, and forget you must,
You drown in sorrow, blinded by lust,

The poison flows, but it's undetected,
You're battered and bruised, and always
      rejected,
But blind you are, to the cold hard truth,
Until one day, he hits the roof,

Down comes the veil, shattering your soul,
You're now not able, to deny the control,
You beg and bargain, with your mind,
"Please let me put this day behind",

Each time you're shattered, you break some
      more,
Until you're unable, to go back to before,
The cracks won't mend, they can't be hidden,

31

You realise true love, here is forbidden,

Once again, you plan your exit,
Your heart is weary, you need to protect it,
This time you see, the damage that's done,
You know, the only way is to run,

You get away, you finally did it,
You somehow manage, to get through it,
He begged and bargained, with your mind,
"Please let me put this day behind",

But you're strong and clear and know the
    truth,
Their words mean nothing, nor their abuse,
Now they're the shell, that they made you,
They are now nothing, but you're back
    to you.

THE CACTUS'S STORY (WHEN HE'S GONE).

Edge and confusion,
pain and despair,
The air isn't clear
The flowers not there.

I'll stay low and hidden,
I'll not make a stand,
The air isn't light,
The loves not around.

I'm watered and noticed,
I'm placed into view,
The air isn't fertile,
"The plants reflects you".

I'm stagnant and stunted,
I'm stuck at the root,
The air isn't graceful,
The truth is on mute.

I'm starting to wither,
I may not survive,
The air isn't lively,
Life cannot thrive.

I'm waving the white,
I'm almost decayed,
The air suffocates me,
The soul is away.

Then one day the air,
Becomes clear and light,
The love builds up brightly,
Growth is in sight.

I feel myself rising,
Like never before,
I've blossomed with grace,
With the truth I will soar.

"Who knew a small cactus,
Was watching your pains,
It sees that you're happy,
So a flower it gains".

HIM (THE ONE THAT GOT AWAY)

I didn't love him,
I loved the bombs he planted,
They exploded into my self-hatred so well.

I didn't love him,
I loved the rejection,
It mirrored back how I always rejected
    myself.

I didn't love him,
I loved the fake apologies,
They gave me hope that I'm worthy of love
    after all.

I didn't love him,

I loved the mask he wore,
He could be anyone I wanted.

I didn't love him,
I loved the part he played,
He could be anything I wanted.

I didn't love him,
I loved the cruelty,
It matched so well with how cruel I was to
        myself.

I didn't love him,
I loved the pain,
It reminded me of inside my own heart.

He created the perfect symphony that played
        throughout my damaged soul.

I didn't love him,
As I didn't love myself.

But I turned his poison into the most potent
        medicine on Earth, and used it to cure
        myself of every pain inside my heart.

I never loved him.

But now,
I will always love myself.

So to him, I say thank you.

You shattered my soul, so I had to learn how
to put it back together.

I crushed the bombs you planted and
moulded them into divine bricks, to build
my strong new boundaries.

I took all the rejection and flipped it into self-
acceptance.

I took your fake apologies and created the
biggest, most authentic apology,
and gave it to myself.

I took the mask you wore, and studied it.

So I see through all masks now, and will
never be deceived again.

I took your cruelty and changed it into kindness and compassion.

I turned the pain you gave me, into strength and unconditional love.

So I've changed my mind,

I do love you.

I love you for helping me become the powerful, divine alchemist that I am today.

Because of you,

I do unto others that which I done unto myself.

So, I want you to know that your cruelty is turning the world into a better place.

You'll be sad to hear.

Yours truly,

The one that got away.

All triggers within these types of relationships have the purpose to make known what we need to heal. They have usually been set up by our souls to help us awaken to our true essence.

Our original core wounds from childhood cause continual triggers within our relationships in adulthood, mirroring back the same patterns and cycles, until they are acknowledged and healed at the root. It is common for starseeds and lightworkers to experience very dysfunctional circumstances around relationships from birth, and usually go on to repeatedly choose abusive partners as part of their mission to awaken. It is within overcoming this pain and suffering that they are birthed into the powerful healer that they came here to be.

Unfortunately, the path of healing and awakening is most often a very lonely path. Partly because, when we awaken, we can suddenly realise that we have been surrounded by toxic relationships for most of our lives, and partly because we find ourselves on a completely different frequency to everyone around us which can feel uncomfortable, and even painful, causing a strong urge to avoid the company of others, which can be isolating and confusing, specifically at the beginning stages of awakening.

As we progress on our journey we not only find peace in our aloneness but we also become more skilled at protecting our energy so we aren't as strongly affected by others. Most often than not we also end up peacefully accepting the end of many relationships and find new ones that are more in resonance with our new state of being.

Once I finally made the courageous decision to let go of what was not for my highest good and heal myself, I began the ultimate journey of self-healing and self-love.

But first came death.

MY MESSAGE

The world became, more than I could take,
One night I lay, with agony and ache,
That moment I chose, not to go on,
I surrendered my case, I was gone,

When death came, the sky was bright,
The walls of my cell fall, to show the light,
I'd never felt, so alive,
When death came, I was revived,

In they came, floating with grace,
Humorous, kind, a charismatic face,
She knew I, and I knew she,
No words were spoken, all I felt was glee,

A million downloads, I understood each one,
The smiling and knowing, it's been so long,
The relief and joy, no longer I suffer,
Death is so easy, did I discover,

Then came the hard part, I came back,
Came back with more, at first, I felt lack,
A birthing of new, a journey of terror,
I felt so alone, but we were together,

I chose this pain, I chose this story,
You'd never believe, what came before me,
It's vast, it's cosmic, it's beyond compre-
     hension,
We're all from the stars, didn't I mention?

Earth is a blip, on an infinite ride,
You may feel alone, but they're right by your
     side,
Life's just a thread, on a cosmic weave,
You come in, you live, and then you leave,

So don't overthink it, don't be a fool,
Find peace in the chaos, that's the real jewel,
It's not what you think, it's not that at all,

You're vast light and love, you know you're
    not small,

So take it from someone who's meant to be
    dead,
It's time to drop fear, and hold up your head,
Fill up with light, take a deep breath,
This is my message from my day of death.

PART TWO
HEALING

They say you must die before you can truly live.

This is definitely true in my case.

This death experience was the beginning of my true life.

A life full of magic and light.

But what comes next on the journey to the light?

Healing, of course.

Healing inside the darkness.

We must look inside of ourselves for all the pain that we hide and suppress. We get very good at pushing our pain to the side to live a 'happy life'. Only until our pain is triggered leading us back into chaos once again.

THE PAIN THAT HIDES

It's in there somewhere, you're not sure
where,
You don't feel it, but a lot you care,
It's compressed and pushed, down so deep,
But sometimes the poison, starts to seep,

When it does, you try to run,
You don't want to feel it, not even a crumb,
You deny it's power, you deny it's there,
It's hidden inside, and it's not to share,

Like a heavy burden, such a high hill,
But from the outside, it's invisible,
You hold it so close, this you can bare,
The worst you can think of, is to share,

"Shhhh."

"Stay hidden from sight, it's safe that way",
But now and then, comes a frightful day,
The poison pours, there's no way out,
You can't run now, you remember what it's
*   about,*

You face the story, you feel the pain,
But only a part, or you'll go insane,
You know one day, healing will come,
But until then, you'll continue to run,

You know you must, dig to the core,
But you know each dig, will only bring more,
You're not sure if, your soul can manage,
But one day you know, you'll recover the
*   damage,*

Until then, you'll try to heal,
Each day you live, breaking from the wheel,
You make a vow, to dig to the core,
Bit by bit, until the pain is no more.

Where do you dig to find the hidden pain?

Into the darkness, of course.

Into the big black hole.

THE BIG BLACK HOLE

It's over there, go on in,
It's dark and deep, and full of sin,
The pain and terror, it judges not,
It's only goal, is to heal a lot,

Once you choose, to take the plunge,
You get pulled in, amongst the gunge,
You fear that, you won't get out,
You must trust the process, with no doubt,

It's not pretty, it's not bright,
You can easily, loose sight,
Sometimes it feels, that it won't end,
But keep the faith, you're on the mend,

For the pain, to turn to light,
Inside the black hole, you must fight,
The more you feel, the end draws near,
Be there for a day, and not for a year,

Accept the darkness, it's your friend,
Have faith that it, will come to an end,
It's there to learn, and heal your soul,
So dive right in, to the big black hole,

You soon learn, not to fear,
Your pain is waiting, lend your ear,
When you do, the pain will come,
Ride the wave, and wait for the sun,

Who'd of guessed, the hole was light,
Disguised with darkness, a gloomy night,
It's full of treasure, for your soul,
Hunt for healing, make that your goal,

It's over there, go on in,
Now you know, there is no sin,
The pain and terror, is illusion you see,
Only love, will set you free.

Only love will set you free.

You need to learn to love yourself.

Only then, can you be free and live in love.

In love with yourself.

Which means you can love everyone else.

How can we start to love ourselves?

Well,

The first step is to see the ego for what it is.

The voice that tells you to pretend you're ok.

The voice that tells you to ignore your own needs.

The voice that tells you to keep your pain hidden.

Unheard, unseen, and numb.

NOT THIS TIME

When it starts to break through,
like weeds, on a cracked pavement,
ego, begging you to turn back,
you ignore it, and carry on,

"Not this time",
you whisper,
this time, I choose to be brave,
I won't keep it down,
I won't pretend anymore,

I know now,
that my strength, is weakness,
being vulnerable, is not the enemy,
it's time to heal.

Hidden beneath the polished surface,
are ugly roots,
dark,
strong,
waiting to split the fragile veneer,
and once again, be at large,

This time,
they won't be sprayed with poisonous denial,
and killed off,
until they choose to rise again,

This time,
they'll be seen, heard and tended to,
until they blossom with brightness,
and become what they never thought
    they'd be.

But first, comes darkness,
the kind of darkness, that has an end,
darkness,
that suffocates the roots,
until the weeds can't climb again.

This darkness,
allows sunlight to pierce through,
bathing all with warmth and acceptance,
and leaving space,
to plant a seed of new beginnings.

I f we stop listening to the ego, we can start to acknowledge and feel our pain, which starts the process of healing. The ego's main job is to keep us safe and comfortable, despite this causing us more harm in the long term. Therefore, it is to be listened to with discernment if we want to break away from existing and start truly living instead.

We can heal ourselves through simple acknowledgement of our pain, consciously feeling it wherever it's location within our body. Staying fully present in that pain with our focus and consciousness without resistance until it transmutes and dissolves.

Once we heal our trauma on a deep level, new triggers cannot ignite that same pain ever again. Focusing on alleviating symptoms with unhelpful coping strategies or bypassing our difficult emotions with denial and avoidance won't heal the cause and the cycle will continue until the root is cleared and healed. As mentioned above, a simple way to do this is using our intention, conscious awareness and presence.

It is vital that we make a commitment to ourselves to heal and unlearn everything we were taught and made to believe, about life, ourselves and the world around us. We must take full responsibility of our suffering, without blaming or judgement and finally take back our power.

IT'S ON YOU

When you're lost in this world,
trying to find the right place,
to thread a piece of your soul,
into the tapestry of life,

Remember.

It's on you.

When you're struck with awe,
from a hue of colour in the sky,
after a rainy afternoon,

Remember.

It's on you.

When your weary legs collapse,
and you're laid on the cold tiled floor,
wondering how,
you'll ever stand again,

Remember.

It's on you.

When you feel the power rise within,
pulling you up,
showing you,
the way out of the darkness,

Remember.

It's on you.

When you finally find the courage,
to thread a piece of your soul,
into the tapestry of life,

Remember.
It's ALL on you.

No one is coming to save you. You are here to heal and save yourself.

If pain comes, you chose it.

If bliss comes, you chose it.

Accept each emotion without resistance.

Feel it, honour it, and transmute it into love with your divine PRESENCE and POWER.

Remember, It's ALL on you.

PART THREE
AWAKENING

In today's world, the truth about Earth and the origins of humanity are hidden from the masses keeping us in a low vibration. The good news is that this age old reality is now being dissolved with the significant amount of light flooding into the Earth, which will allow humanity to ascend to a higher density.

Along with the obvious wealth imbalance, and other manipulations in our lives, a big part of this frequency control on Earth preventing mass awakening is the constant promotion of the importance of material wealth and physical beauty. These are promoted to be seen as the key to happiness and success, mainly using 'celebrities' to distracts the masses from their true nature and power. This keeps them in a very superficial and disconnected state of being, therefore preventing them the from remembering who they really are.

To live more in resonance with our souls purpose it is vital that we unlearn everything we have been taught and forge our own path away from the manipulation of mainstream ideologies. We must become immune to the bombardment of these distractions and false information about what's good for our health, how we should think, what we should look like or what we should buy. This will allow us to create own way of being and help us achieve unshakable peace and happiness without the need for such meaningless distractions.

Raising our frequency is the most important element needed to claim back our power and be at the forefront of the revolution.

It's coming, it's here, and nothing can stop it.

THE MODERN CON

This modern world, is not real I see,
Everyone's living, a fantasy,
Some they think, that all is right,
Then others they know, but they fight,

They fight against, what they know is true,
They cheat themselves, they don't know
    who,
Don't know who they are, so they start to
    pour,
Pour things and all, and only want more,

Pour into themselves, to cover what's below,
Below the surface, until truth starts to show,

Once it does, there's no way out,
You must face yourself, that's what it's all
about.

When you face yourself, hell will come,
But nothing's more painful, than staying
hidden from the sun,
The suns light will, burn and burn,
It is the only way, this you learn,

Once all has burned, though the night,
You've been through darkness, alone you
fight,
The other side, not many is there,
You'll continue alone, but this you can bare,

Bare the aloneness, and the real journey
starts,
You start to help others, to open their hearts,
There's no way back, you wouldn't want
to go,
This is where you belong, this you know.

You soon learn, you're not alone,
They've been there, since before day one,

These are who, get you through this life,
Without them this world, would cut like a
*   knife,*

They're rooting for you, you must know,
You're stronger than most, no matter
*   how low,*
You've been to valleys, and mountain tops,
The cycle continues, it never stops,

What stops is the pain, that others give,
You rise up higher, and you live,
You live for others, you live for yourself,
No one can rock you, not even with stealth.

You live alone, but peace you find,
You leave hell, and pain behind,
It's served you well, but now it's gone,
Wake up and see, this world is a con,

What matters most, is love for yourself,
Love for others, that's the only wealth,
The only wealth, that you need,
So free yourself, from all the greed,

The greed of this world, will destroy all,
You must rise above this, and stand tall,
Stand tall against, all that's not true,
This is the only way, that leads back to YOU!

THE DIFFERENCE

Life is a dream of reality,
But reality seems like a dream to me,

Full of beauty, full of pain,
Sometimes I hope it's not all in vain,

Through the good times and the bad,
Flowing along in this world that's mad,

It's hard to stay above the waves,
Smile, don't be the one that caves,

Don't let them win, don't let them soar,
Just be happy knowing less is more,

Never forget what matters the most,
Sometimes that takes you to be at your
    lowest,

As we come so we go,
But love still matters even though this is so,

So shine your light every day,
Make a difference so they say.

THEM

You see them,
wherever you go,
they know not who they are,

Blank expressions,
waiting to be led,
they care not by whom,

You see them,
avoiding all they can,
they know not why,

Eyes deadened,
unable to see,
they care not at all,

You see them,
ignoring all that's true,
they see not what they should,

Hearts weak,
with heavy burdens,
they feel it not,

You see them,
using poison to get by,
no hope they have,

Stomachs churning,
with all of life's troubles,
peace they will never find,

You see them, lost,
not wanting to be found,
lost, they will remain,

Souls crushed,
unable to rise again,
joy, they will never feel,

You see them,
surviving,
existing,
dead.

Don't be them.

Earth and the human collective can appear so dark and hopeless on the surface, however, paradoxically, this darkness and extensive suffering is the exact state that can help humanity evolve into a higher state of consciousness.

It is humanities gift, that most never open.

All it takes is that one moment when the soul wakes up and says NO MORE!

Only then can the fire within begin to rise.

FIRE

It's roaring and wild,
in an open field,
You fear it's power,
that you wish to wield,

If you run, you will never learn,
You can't feel the magic,
without feeling the burn,

So you sit, and you feel,
let the flames overcome,
Surrendering to,
the power for the sun,

Surrender, then causes,
the fire to burst,
Up through each chakra,
purification first,

It rises up, roaring inside,
Splitting in half,
let go you decide,

Formless you are,
you feel it now,
You master the heat,
the flames you allow,

Engulfed in the flames,
potential is near,
You be-come the fire,
your path now is clear,

So wield the wild fire,
let it roar through your soul,
Let the magic flow through,
without your control,

STORMS OF LIGHT:

It's roaring and wild,
but this time it's you,
The fire is now yours,
many dreams to peruse.

S urrender to the wild fire within.

Allow yourself to awaken to your ultimate potential and realise what you really are.

Devine fire,

Light.

THE LIGHT WITHIN

It starts out bright,
perfect and sweet,
We come here knowing,
then the world we greet,

As we go on,
through this Earth,
Our light slowly dampens,
and so does our worth,

They don't mean to,
their lights have gone out,
They might be neglectful,
or they might shout,

You don't understand,
it causes you pain,
Your light continues,
to dim and wane,

Then comes school,
dimmed lights together,
The teachers don't help,
there's just no shelter,

Everyone's lost,
wandering in the dark,
Lost on this Earth journey,
we continue to walk,

Adulthood,
it only gets worse,
Your light is out,
nothing to disperse,

Some they can't,
bare the dark,
They use what they can,
their pain is stark,

STORMS OF LIGHT:

Everyone's lost,
they know not what they do,
You start to wonder,
how to get back to you,

The you that's bright,
perfect and sweet,
You wish you could,
have a clean sheet,

Then you remember,
why you came,
You find that spark,
and remember the game,

It's meant to be fun,
joyous and free,
But when the lights out,
you just can't see,

You begin the real journey,
inward you go,
You re-light that spark,
then others you show,

You finally have,
something to disperse,
From now it gets better,
you're free from the curse,

Your light starts shining,
even others can see,
Others start to wonder,
"maybe that's also for me",

You inspire all,
with your newfound light,
Your wisdom, your courage,
and your insight,

All it takes,
is that one spark,
That's how a person,
can make their mark,

So shine your light,
for others to see,
To make their way home,
So they can be free.

TREES TALK

Living in a man made forest,
the shield,
that blocks us, from our home.

Most like it,
it's entertaining,
and can be fun,
but it's not like home.

The comfort kills,
any last spark we have.

We get lost,
in the world of inverted nature.

They created man made nature,
to heal, it only
kills.

What's wrong with nature itself?

It's fine as it is.

I woke up one day.

I swam through a murky sea,
of plastic and poison,

I climbed the man-made trees,
that kill and cause disease,

I crawled through the viciously sprayed mud,
that houses the shadows of our survival,

All whilst breathing the air,
that is now poison itself.

But I made it.

I sat by an ancient tree.

"Where have you been?", she said.
It took you long enough.

"I've been lost", I replied.

"Lost dear?"

Yes, but I'm home now.

M any on the awakening journey begin to feel a deep longing to 'go home' without being sure exactly where that is or what that means. This is due an unconscious remembrance of our home beyond 3rd density Earth but also due to the low vibrational frequencies of Earth becoming more noticeable once you have awakened to a higher frequency. Everything can suddenly feel more painful and intolerable in the early stages of awakening, but rest assured, this most certainly gets better as time goes on once you integrate your growth and find new meaning and purpose.

It is important to accept and love our home here on Earth, after all it is our home for now. This will give us the roots and grounding we need to fully connect to our true home beyond Earth. Both elements are needed to propel us to higher frequencies and carry out our mission to its full potential.

Although, from experience I am very aware this is no easy task.

ENLIGHTENMENT

The ever elusive,
Just out of reach,
You long for its lessons,
That it has to teach.

You think it erases,
The human in you,
But the more you enlighten,
The human comes through.

You have for infinity,
To be an enlightened soul,
You're here to enjoy,
The journey to whole.

You're not here to sit,
And run away home,
So be here with presence,
On the Earth that you roam.

You've been enlightened,
Many times than you know,
So engulf in duality,
What seeds will you sow.

It's all up to you,
No future is a given,
Infinite facets,
Choose which one to live in.

It's not in the stars,
The cosmos ain't here,
It's right where you are,
It's now, always near.

You think it's extraordinary,
You think it's profound,
Stop thinking and seeking,
And it will be found.

STORMS OF LIGHT:

It is, and you are,
I am that I am,
It's now and it's here,
Don't fall for the scam.

Find profoundness in simplicity, find extraordinary in the ordinary and you will truly enlighten.

Humanity is finding their light and standing in their power.

Unlearning everything they've been told about who they are or how to live.

The Earth is flooding with unstoppable light.

What a journey it has been, and so may it continue.

Nothing can stop what's coming.

WE'RE ALL HERE NOW

A lifetime of pain, sadness and grief,
Alone on the earth, wandering in disbelief,
It seems you're alone, the only one,
All you know, is that you're not home.

After a while, the suffering ends,
Upgrades and light codes, your family sends,
You can now bare, the earth as it is,
But you're still alone, in this life that you live.

Then out comes your family, right here on
    Earth,
All here for the light, a duty to serve,
It's time to join forces, and close the dark
    gates,

We know the lights near, Eden awaits.

The light is strong, it's already won,
The darkness descending, can only block out
    the sun,
So all join together, we're all here now,
Smash through our mission, then take a
    bow.

This is the reason, we came here for,
To transmute the darkness, and hear the light
    roar,
The power and love, that your light does
    hold,
Is the New Earth story, that's waiting to be
    told!

PART FOUR
THE LIGHT

I eventually found my light, remembered my mission and 'cured' my 'lifelong, incurable illnesses'. I achieved what I was told was impossible and so can you with whatever obstacle you are up against in life.

The only thing I have ever truly aimed for in life is inner peace, and I finally have this in abundance. The life I live now is beyond anything I could have imagined when looking back at where I've been.

Unshakable peace and happiness is the only goal I will ever prioritise, this what you can achieve when you heal yourself and listen to your soul, not what you've been taught and made to believe by a world that doesn't understand what a soul needs to be free.

THE VOID

A space so vast, with nothing to see,
No safety or knowing, no you nor me,
A place of discomfort, a place of despair,
You've entered the void, your soul it will tare.

A space in the middle, with no right or
    wrong,
No language or sound, no words and no song,
A place of transition, a place of renew,
You've entered the void, where you will
    find you,

A space of aloneness, with no one around,
No connection or beings, no bond to be bound,
A place of solitude, a place of reflection,

You've entered the void, you're at the cross
section,

A space of creation, and vast potential,
No definite answer, the right one's not
essential,
A place of silence, a place of rebirth,
You've entered the void, what will you
unearth,

A space where you realise, the answers you
seek,
Redirection is here, be it year or a week,
You feel the dense fall, for the new to become,
You're out of the void, you rediscovered
the sun,

A new reality, created from scratch,
You entered the egg and awaited to hatch,
A canvas that's blank, make it what you will,
The void is transition, a new life to fulfil,

A new truth to behold, found deep in the void,
A place of discovery, not a place to avoid,
The pain and discomfort, has so much to
show,

Stay present and peaceful, no matter
    how low,

A new transition, only until the next,
Make it simple, or make it complex,
The choice is yours, in all that you are,
Chose pain and discomfort, to be near or far,

Each moment the truth, is deep in your heart,
The void comes in close, to remind and
    restart,
Find comfort in darkness, find you in the
    pain,
For the void is the answer, and you'll go there
    again.

Y ou may wonder why I placed the void within the light.

Well, the void is the birthplace of creation, the very place where light is born. The void can be a painful, yet transformative and enlightening place. It is a place we will visit repeatedly on our awakening journey, usually each time we fall out of alignment with our current circumstances and it's time to birth a new direction.

When the void comes into your life, get excited, not resistive. Let it ignite your wonder and anticipation of what's to come on the other side. Feel and accept whatever discomfort arises and be open to learn all of the lessons it has to teach, while you await the birth of a new phase in your life.

This in how we master duality.

M any brave souls are overcoming their darkness and basking in the expansive state of duality.

Many sparks have been lit across the Earth.

We are finally awakening en masse, relishing in this deep and profound emotional human experience and living as the sovereign beings we're meant to be.

By raising our frequencies, being present in our pain and standing against what isn't in alignment with our soul, we step into our power and help others do the same.

This is how we create the new Earth.

The Earth's ascension is upon us.

What a time to be alive.

"Here's my cosmic story".

"This is my story",

"The fire,

The spirit,

The soul,

The light,

The angel,

The galactic,

The creator,

The awareness,

The consciousness.

The

I AM".

THE LAW

I AM,
And will always be,

So just be,
Where you are,

You are,
That is all,

You are all,
And all is you,

You are one,
We are one,

One is all,
All is one,

That's the law of one.

EDEN (SEEDS FROM THE STARS)

Paradise was created, Earth was made,
All they needed, was the perfect way,
Made with perfection, pi and light,
The vehicle to take them, was in sight,

The game was set, the play was planned,
In they go, to the paradise land,
Gave up their knowing, willingly,
To learn their lessons, until they are free,

They thought it would be easy, full of fun,
But when they arrived, they were overrun,
They got stuck, karma encased,
What became of the human race?

After a while, emergency raised,
The call went out, "humans to be saved!",
There was plenty, who came to see,
Wanted to be part, of the revolutionary,

In we came, seeds from the stars,
But first, fast tracked through our own Earth
    scars,
We took on more, than we could bare,
To regain our light, so we could share,

We took on all, to break the karmic wheel,
Lessons to learn, many layers to peel,
We knew how dark, Earth would be,
But it didn't make it, at all easy,

We came with love, we came with light,
As you can see, the end is in sight,
The world is healing, souls are free,
It'll soon be fun, and even easy,

Darkness is lifting, first the ego will fight,
It's all part of our journey, back to the light,
So don't be resistive, don't stay being small,
Paradise is coming, it'll be there for all.

ALIEN

Here on Earth, it's been so long,
you sometimes think you're human,
a little too much, of the day to day,
and you slip right into Truman.

A break you need, from the noise and lights,
to get back to who you are,
it doesn't take much, of the sacred breath,
for the light warrior to roar.

Another dimension comes to see,
how you're doing in this life,
they show you just enough of love,
but too much will cut like a knife.

Too much of home, is too much to bare,
when you're here on Earth to stay,
they wish you well and stay close by,
knowing you'll be back with them one day.

But for now, your missions set,
Earth it is for duty,
a turbulent place that's filled with pain,
but oh my gosh the beauty.

You came here knowing,
how tough it is, to be here in 3D,
they talk of heaven and of hell,
both is here, they just can't see.

So just remember every day,
to find that light inside,
you're only human for a while,
so just enjoy the ride.

PART FIVE
HOME

Home beyond Earth.

We will return.

COSMIC NECTAR

Hollow the apple and jump inside,
A golden globe of splenda,
A soothing light, all around,
Paint a picture of the cosmic nectar.

Look up at the core, a portal beyond,
With cubes carved into the fruit,
They spiral out, in sacred perfection,
You soon hear a fine cosmic flute.

The music sends joy, flowing into your soul,
Then bliss bubbles up more and more,
Each time that you move, the bliss overflows,
The cosmic nectar drips out of the core.

You laugh and you smile, at the bubbles
of joy,
Let the feeling of ecstasy rise,
Each wiggle and giggle, causes joy to explode,
The cosmic nectar is the ultimate prize.

WHERE YOU BELONG

A place,
not quite here,
yet not quite there,

connected to all,
yet connected to none,

you can't quite feel it,
yet you feel it completely,

And you always know, it's where you belong.

A place,
that can't be found,
yet find it you will,

in another dimension,
yet close by it is,

no memory you have,
yet you remember it fully,

And you always know, it's where you belong.

A place,
where you've always lived,
yet have been gone forever,

its shimmering lights,
can't be seen in the dark,

you know how to get there,
but lost you feel,

And you always know, it's where you belong.

A place,
that sings,
yet can't be heard,

full of love,
that can't be felt,

It's waiting for you,
you're waiting for it,

And you always know, it's where you belong.

A place,
that has no words,
yet silent it's not,

form doesn't exist,
yet plenty to see,

many times you visit,
yet you recall it not,

And you always know, it's where you belong.

A place,
of nothingness,
yet filled with love,

you never left,
within you it lies,

it's in your heart,
it's in your soul,

And you know you will always return.

CAN YOU REMEMBER?

Golden light,
moulded into magnificence,
with indigo and magenta jewels,
that shimmer, sing and hum,
swaying in a gentle breeze of nothingness.

Can you remember?

It's where you're from,
it's where you're going,
and it's where you will always be.

Through the portal,
from one realm to another,
you travel with an inner smile,

that deepens inside your formless being,
as you speed closer to you aim.

Can you remember?

It's where you remain,
no matter where you are,
and you will never leave.

They greet you,
with the most gleeful celebration,
familiar, comforting,
you feel the deepest knowingness,
that this is your home.

Can you remember?

It's where your cosmic family awaits,
bursting with pride, with longing,
and of course, with love.

Each breath,
brings a sympathy of the most harmonious
     music,
that only a soul can hear,
the sound creates blissful ripples,

throughout your entire being.

Can you remember?

It's where your soul belongs,
it's where it was before,
and it's where it resides eternally.

Crowds of fireflies,
glistening with excitement,
surrounding your return,
all to know of your Earthy travels,
no words are spoken, but the story is received
  with awe.

Can you remember?

It's where you long to be,
it's where your soul was born,
and it's where you will always return.

FAR FROM HOME

She's from the stars, there is no doubt,
A cosmic past of darkness,
She's far from home, but stay she must,
To take away the sharpness.

Here from afar, to soften the world,
With alchemy and light,
Alone she feels, among the trees,
But the grid she must ignite.

The pain it comes, from deep within,
This pain she chose with bravery,
She got a chance, to leave this world,
But back she came to slavery.

The mission is clear, choose love for all,
Despite the pain they give you,
She understands, their hidden pain,
Forgiveness is a virtue.

She longs for home, dreams of the light,
Meets family through the portal,
It's not the same, but enough to stay,
"Thank god I'm not immortal".

The Earth she loves, the people too,
But she knows, she doesn't belong,
She feels it fully, every day,
Dreaming of the stars sweet song.

What keeps her here, is the promise of,
Her home with the golden light,
She feels the music, inside her heart,
So she stays here with all her mite.

When it's time to go, she'll have no fear,
She's been to death before,
It's full of light, love and compassion,
"But I'll stay here a little bit more".

ABOUT THE AUTHOR

Stepf Greener is a writer and poet, the author of Storms of Light: A Cosmic Awakening. She is a multidimensional healer and also a qualified psychiatric nurse who left her nursing career in 2022 to move into alternative healing.

Stepf is a 35 year old single mother of 2 children who are 12 and 14. She lives with her children in Sunderland, UK. She was left as a single mother in her early twenties when her children were 1 week old and 1 year old. Determined to give her children a decent life she went to college and university to train as a psychiatric nurse when the children were babies, out of necessity to financially provide for them. Her experiences of what is known as mental illness led her to her psychiatric nursing career as she wanted to help others who may be experiencing the same as her. After qualifying as a nurse and being promoted in her career, Stepf left her job as a senior nurse in mainstem healthcare to open her own business providing alternative healing.

Stepping away from fulltime work enabled Stepf to have the mind space and time to finally integrate her own healing gifts and heal herself in a way she never thought was possible. What are said to be severe/disabling, life-long and incurable illnesses, only to be controlled with strong, sedative medication which is advised to be taken for life, were completely healed within months of Stepf activating her gifts and healing herself after decades of significant disruptions.

After Stepf remembered her true origins and mission on Earth she came to realise that her severe 'illnesses' and experiences of terrifying altered states during her awakening, along with the multiple death/near-death experiences were all part of her initiation to become the healer she is today. She knows now that her experiences are connected to her divine purpose here helping with the birth of the new Earth.

Stepf is the founder of Cosmic Soul Healing and uses Celestial Shamanism and Multidimensional Healing to help clients all over the world heal, awaken and remember who they are. Her main goal is to activate and initiate others into the high frequency energies that she has been able to access during her awakening journey which she does within her Cosmic Gateway Activation Programs and Events giving others the power to heal themselves and others in a deep and magical way.

Stepf believes that many of us are here to help rid the Earth of the low vibrational energies that humanity has existed in for millennia, and are here to help humanity claim back their sovereignty and remember that they are;

Creators, with God source energy and vast cosmic origins.

> *It is time for humanity to rise, take back their power and remember who they really are".*

You can find Stepf and her services via the links below and subscribe to her website for future book launches.

Website https://www.cosmicsoulhealing.net

facebook.com/stepfanie.greener
instagram.com/cosmic_soul_awakening